Semiconductors and PN Junction Diode

Semiconductors are materials that are neither completely insulators nor completely conductors. Some of the most important semiconductor devices are diodes, transistors, and thyristors. These semiconductor devices have changed the face of electronics today. Semiconductors find wide applications because of their compactness, reliability, and low cost. They can handle a wide range of current and voltage. One of the most important reasons of choosing diodes, transistors, thyristors or any other semiconductor device is their ability to be integrated into complex but readily manufactured modules.

This chapter deals with fundamentals of semiconductors and PN Junction diode such as

☞ Definitions of Matter – Atom – Element – Molecule – Compound
☞ Atomic Structure and Neil Bohr's Atomic Theory
☞ Energy Band/Energy Level for Conductors, Insulators and Semiconductors
☞ Properties of semiconductor
☞ classification of Semiconductors
☞ Intrinsic Semiconductor and Extrinsic Semiconductor
☞ N-type Semiconductor and P-type Semiconductor
☞ Effect of Temperature on Semiconductors
☞ PN Junction Diode and its Formation
☞ Diode Biasing: Forward Biased Condition and Reverse Biased Condition
☞ V-I Characteristics of Diode
☞ PN Junction Diode Equation
☞ 5 Effect of Temperature on Diode Current
☞ Ratings/Specifications of a Diode
☞ Ideal and Real view of a Diode
☞ Applications of PN Junction Diode: Diode as a Switch and Diode as Half Wave Rectifier
☞ Zener diode
☞ V-I Characteristics of Zener Diode
☞ Avalanche breakdown and Zener breakdown
☞ Applications of Zener diode: Zener Diode as a Voltage Regulator

Matter – Atom – Element – Molecule – Compound

Matter: Matter is any substance which has mass and occupies its own space. It may exists in solids, liquids, gases or plasma state

Atom: Smallest particle of an element is called atom. It is made of a central nucleus containing protons and neutrons. The electrons revolve around the nucleus in different imaginary paths called orbits or shells.

Element: Group of similar atoms is called element. It cannot be further resolved into simpler substances by chemical means. Eg: Copper, gold, silicon etc

Molecule: Group of two or more similar elements combining together is called molecule. Eg H_2, O_2 Na_3 etc

Compound: Group of similar or dissimilar elements combining together is called compound. Eg H_2o, $NaCl$, H_2SO_4 etc

1.1 Atomic Structure

As per modern atomic structure, the mass of an atom and its positive charge are concentrated in a tiny nucleus, while negatively charged electrons revolve around the nucleus in elliptical orbits. The central nucleus contains positively charged protons and neutral neutrons. The below figure gives the picture of atomic structure

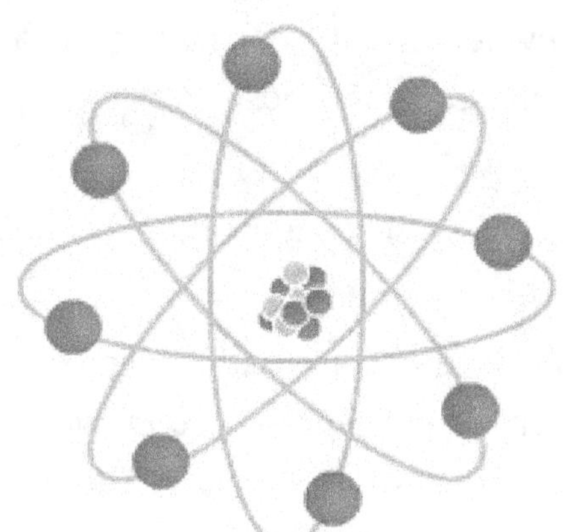
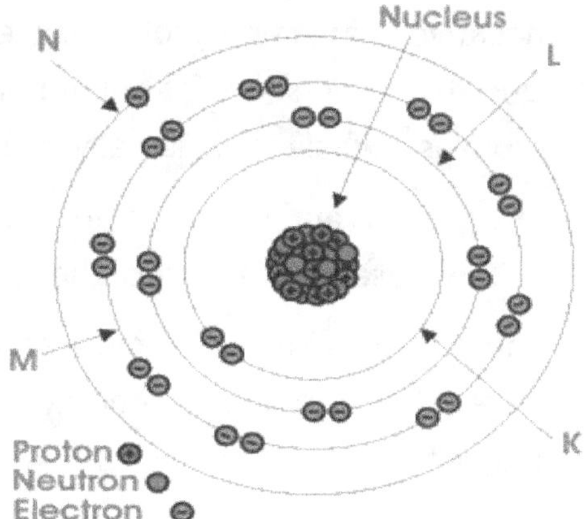

It is found that a proton is 1840 times heavier than an electron. The absolute value of electric charge of a proton and of an electron is same. So there must be same number of protons and electrons in an electrically neutral atom. The orbits along which the electrons revolve are also known as shells/energy levels. In atomic structure the successive shells are named as K, L, M, N, O, P, and Q as per increasing distance outwards from the nucleus. Each shell or energy level has maximum number of electrons for stability. The maximum number of electron in a shell can be given by the formula

$$N=2n^2$$

Where, N is the number of electrons and

n is the shell number in sequential order outward from the nucleus.

As per the above formula,

☞ The maximum number of electrons in first inner shell from nucleus is $2 \times 1^2 = 2$,

☞ The maximum number of electrons in second inner shell from nucleus is $2 \times 2^2 = 8$,

☞ The maximum number of electrons in third inner shell from nucleus is $2 \times 3^2 = 18$,

and so on.

These values are only applicable for inner shell/energy level of an atomic structure. For outer most shell of an atom the above rule is not applicable. After fulfilling the maximum numbers of electrons in different inner shells, the rest electrons would be in outer most shell of atom.

1.1.1 Neil Bohr's Atomic Theory

In order to explain the stability of an atom, Neils Bohr gave a new arrangement of electrons in the atom in 1913. According to Neil Bohr:

☞ An atom is made up of three particles, electrons, protons and neutrons. Electrons have a negative charge and protons have a positive charge whereas neutrons have no charge. Due to the presence of equal number of negative electrons and positive protons, the atom as a whole is electrically neutral.

☞ The protons and electrons are located in a small nucleus at the center of the atom. Due to the presence of protons, the nucleus is positively charged.

☞ The electrons revolve rapidly around the nucleus in fixed circular paths called energy levels/shells/orbits. The 'energy levels' or 'shells' or 'orbits' are represented in two ways: either by the numbers 1, 2, 3, 4, 5 and 6 or by letters K, L, M, N, O and P. The energy levels are counted from center to outwards.

☞ Each energy level is associated with a fixed amount of energy. The shell nearest to the nucleus has minimum energy and the shell farthest from the nucleus has maximum energy.

☞ There is no change in the energy of electrons as long as they keep revolving with the same energy level. But, when an electron jumps from a lower energy level to a higher one, some energy is absorbed while some energy is emitted.

☞ When an electron jumps from a higher energy level to a lower one, the amount of energy absorbed or emitted is given by the difference of energies associated with the two levels. Thus, if an electron jumps from orbit 1 (energy E_1) to orbit 2 (energy E_2), the change in energy is given by $E_2 - E_1$.

☞ The energy change is accompanied by absorption of radiation energy of $E = E_2 - E_1 = h$ where, h is a constant called 'Planck's constant' and is the frequency of radiation absorbed or emitted. The value of h is 6.626×10^{-34} J·s. The absorption and emission of light due to electron jumps are measured by using spectrometers

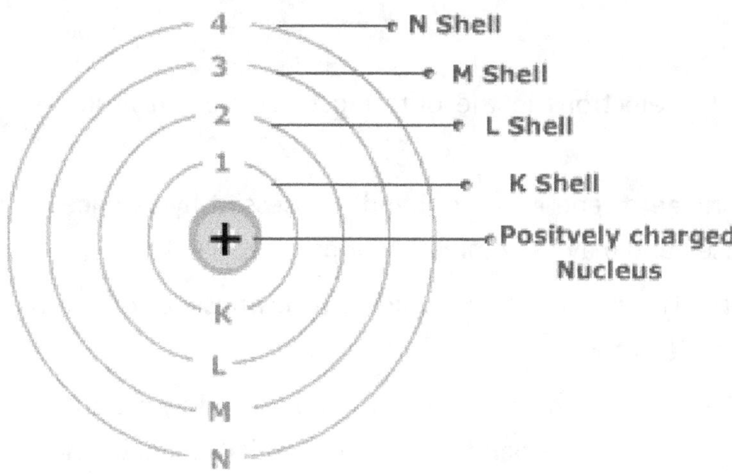

1.1.2 Energy Band/Energy Level

Energy band diagram below shows the levels of energies of electrons in the material. There are two kinds of energy bands and one kind of energy gap. They are

☞ Conduction band

☞ Valance band

☞ Forbidden gap

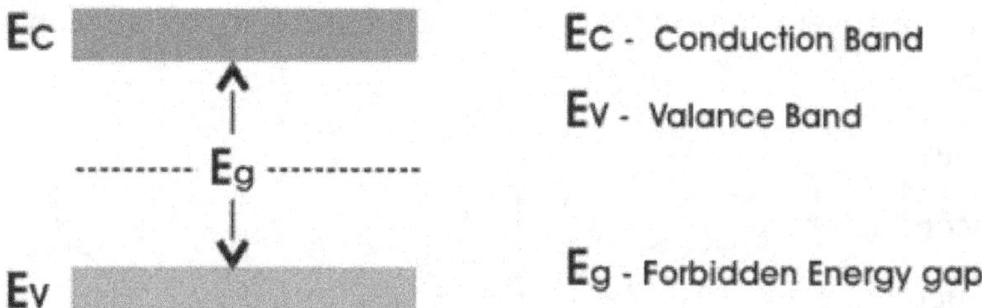

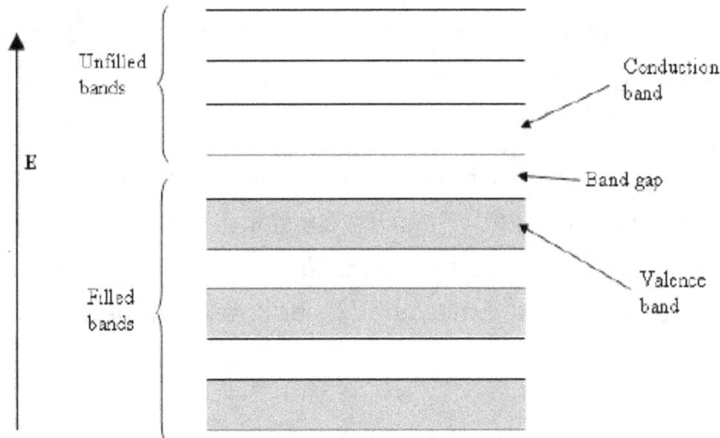

Valence electrons: The electrons in the outermost orbit of an atom are known as valence electrons.

Valence band: The range of energies (i.e. band) possessed by valence electrons is known as valence band. Valence band may be completely or partially filled.

Conduction electrons: The free electrons which are responsible for the conduction of current are called conduction electrons.

Conduction band: The range of energies (i.e. band) possessed by conduction electrons is known as conduction band. Generally, this band is empty or partially filled by the electrons

Forbidden energy gap: The separation between conduction band and valence band on the energy level diagram is known as forbidden energy gap.

1.2 Conductors, Insulators and Semiconductors

The materials can be classified on the basis of energy gap between their valence band and conduction band. The valence band is the band consisting of free valence electron and the conduction band is empty band. Conduction takes place when an electron jumps from valence band to conduction band and the gap between these two bands is energy gap. Wider the gap between the bands, higher the energy it requires to shift the electron to conduction band.

Hence according to electrical conductivity Solid-state materials can be classified into three groups. Such as:

> ➢ Insulator
>
> ➢ Semiconductor
>
> ➢ Conductor

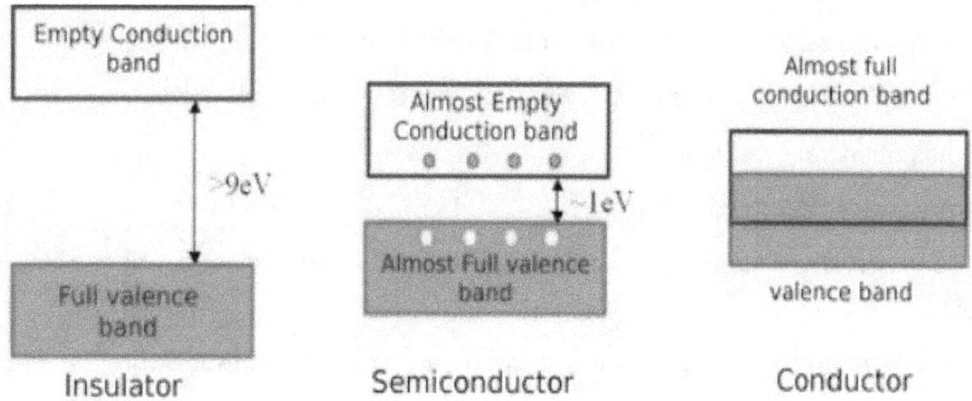

Insulators

Insulators (*e.g.* wood, glass, plastics, rubber etc.) are those substances which do not allow the passage of electric current through them. In terms of energy band, the valence band is full while the conduction band is empty as shown in the above figure. Further, the energy gap between valence and conduction bands is very large (>9 *eV*). Therefore, a very high electric field is required to push the valence electrons to the conduction band. For this reason, the electrical conductivity of such materials is extremely small. An insulator has negative temperature coefficient of resistance.

Conductors

Conductors (*e.g.* copper, aluminum) are those substances which easily allow the passage of electric current through them. It is because there are a large number of free electrons available in a conductor. In terms of energy band as shown in the above figure, the valence and conduction bands overlap each other. Due to this overlapping a slight potential difference across a conductor causes the free electrons to constitute electric current.

Semi-conductors

Semiconductors (*e.g. germanium, silicon etc.*) are those substances whose electrical conductivity lies in between conductors and insulators. In terms of energy band, the valence band is almost filled and conduction band is almost empty as shown in the above figure. Further, the energy gap between valence and conduction bands is very small.

At room temperature, the valence electrons of the Semiconductors do not have enough energy to cross over to the conduction band, acts as insulator. However, when the temperature is raised or external energy is applied, some of the valence electrons may acquire enough energy to cross over to the conduction band, acts as conductor. Hence, the resistance of a Semiconductor decreases with the increase in temperature.

1.2.1 Properties of semiconductor

The main properties of semiconductor are as follows:

☞ Electrical conductivity lies in between conductors and insulators.

☞ It has filled valence band

☞ It has empty conduction band

☞ There is a small energy gap or forbidden gap (1 eV) between valence and conduction bands.

☞ Semiconductor virtually behaves as an insulator at low temperatures and as conductor on applying external energy

☞ Examples are Silicon, Germanium etc

1.2.2 Difference between Conductor, Insulator and Semiconductor

The main differences between conductor, insulator and semiconductor are as follows

Conductor	Insulator	Semiconductor
The conductivity of conductor is very high.	The conductivity of insulator is very low.	The conductivity of semiconductor is moderate.
It has very low resistivity.	It has very high resistivity.	It has moderate resistivity.
It has no forbidden gap.	It has large forbidden gap.	It has small forbidden gap.
Conductor has positive temperature coefficient of resistance.	Insulator has negative temperature coefficient of resistance.	Semiconductor has negative temperature coefficient of resistance
In conductor, both the effect of resistance and temperature are increases	In insulator, effect of resistance is decreases and effect of temperature is increases.	In semiconductor, effect of resistance is decreases and effect of temperature is increases.
There is large number of electrons available for conduction.	There is small number of electrons available for conduction.	There is moderate number of electrons available for conduction.
Examples: Metals, aluminium,	Paper, Mica glass.	Silicon, Germanium.

copper.		

Points to Remember

- ☞ *Energy band of a solid is the large number of energy levels confined in a small region of energy range of a given solid, constitute what is known as energy bands.*
- ☞ *In some solids, there is an energy gap in between the energy bands. This energy gap is called forbidden gap. The energy band above the forbidden gap is called conduction band and the energy band below the forbidden gap is called valence band.*
- ☞ *The conductivity of a solid depends upon the number of electrons present in the conduction band and number of holes present in valence band.*
- ☞ *In metals, the conduction band and valence band partly overlap each other and there is no forbidden energy gap.*
- ☞ *In insulators, the conduction band is empty and valence band is completely filled and forbidden gap is quite large. No electron from valence band can cross over to conduction band at room temperature, even if electric field is applied. Hence there is no conductivity of the insulators.*
- ☞ *In semiconductors, the conduction band is empty and valence band is totally filled. But the forbidden gap between conduction band and valence band is quite small, which is about 1 eV. No electron from valence band can cross over to conduction band. Therefore, the semiconductor behaves as insulator.*
- ☞ *At room temperature, some electrons in the valence band acquire thermal energy, greater than energy gap of 1 eV and jump over to the conduction band where they are free to move under the influence of even a small electric field. Due to which, the semiconductor acquires small conductivity at room temperature.*

1.3 Classification of Semiconductors

The semi-conductors are internally classified as below

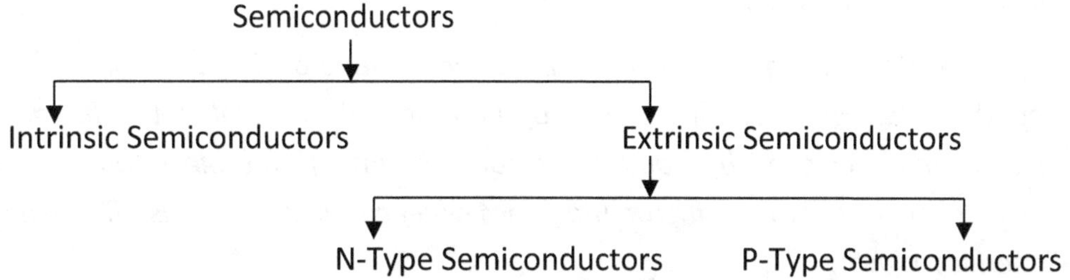

1.3.1 Intrinsic Semiconductor

A semiconductor in an extremely pure form is known as an intrinsic semiconductor. Here flow of electron takes place by increasing the temperature

In this case the holes in the valence band are vacancies created by electrons that have been thermally excited to the conduction band and hole-electron pairs are created. When electric field is applied across an intrinsic semiconductor, the current conduction takes place by *free electrons* and *holes* as shown in the below figure.

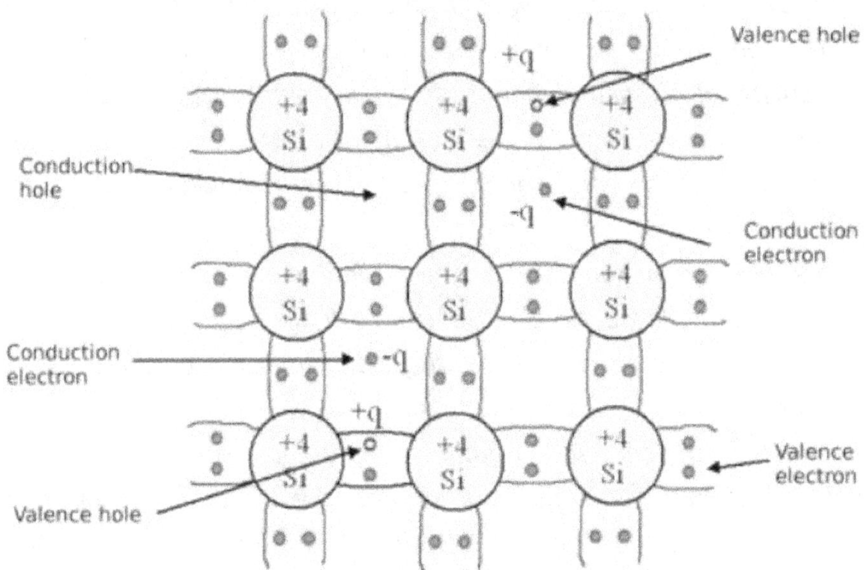

The free electrons are produced due to the breaking up of some covalent bonds by thermal energy. At the same time, holes are created in the covalent bonds. Under the influence of electric field, conduction through the semiconductor is by both free electrons and holes. Therefore, the total current inside the semiconductor is the sum of currents due to free electrons and holes. This creates new holes near the positive terminal which again drift towards the negative terminal.

1.3.2 Extrinsic Semiconductor

An extrinsic semiconductor is an impure semiconductor. Here the pure semiconductor is doped by the addition of small amount of impurity which is able to change its electrical properties. That is achieved by adding a small amount of suitable impurity (having 3 or 5 valence electron) to a semiconductor (having 4 valence electron). It is then called impure or extrinsic semiconductor.

The process of adding impurities to a semiconductor is known as *doping*. The purpose of adding impurity is to increase either the number of free electrons or holes in the semiconductor crystal.

If a pentavalent impurity (having 5 valence electrons) is added to the semiconductor, a large number of free electrons are produced in the semiconductor. Here penta valent impurity is called dopant

If a trivalent impurity (having 3 valence electrons) is added to the semiconductor, large numbers of holes are produced in the semiconductor crystal. Here tri valent impurity is called accepter.

Depending upon the type of impurity added, extrinsic semiconductors are classified into:

- ➢ N-type semiconductor
- ➢ P-type semiconductor

1.3.3 Differences between Intrinsic and Extrinsic Semiconductors

The main differences between intrinsic and extrinsic semiconductors are as follows

Intrinsic Semiconductors	Extrinsic Semiconductors
It is pure semi-conducting material	It is impure semi-conducting material
Impurity atoms are not added	It is prepared by doping a small quantity of impurity atoms to the pure semi-conducting material.
The number of free electrons in the conduction band and the no. of holes in valence band are exactly equal and very small indeed.	The number of free electrons and holes is never equal. There is excess of electrons in n-type semi-conductors and excess of holes in p-type semi-conductors.
Its electrical conductivity is low.	Its electrical conductivity is high.
Its electrical conductivity is a function of temperature alone.	Its electrical conductivity depends upon the temperature as well as on the quantity of impurity atoms doped the structure.
Examples: crystalline forms of pure silicon and germanium.	Examples: silicon "Si" and germanium "Ge" crystals with impurity atoms of As, Sb, P etc. or In B, Aℓ etc.

1.4 N-type Semiconductor

When a small amount of pentavalent impurity is added to a pure semiconductor, it forms N-type semiconductor.

The pentavalent atom has five valence electrons and a pure semiconductor (tetravalent) atom have four valence electrons. The four valence electrons of the pentavalent atom form covalent bonds with the neighboring tetravalent atoms. The fifth electron of the pentavalent atom is available free. This free electron is available in conduction band. Hence the addition of pentavalent impurity provides a large number of free electrons in the semiconductor crystal.

Typical examples of pentavalent impurities are *arsenic, antimony, Bismuth and Phosphorous etc.* Such impurities which produce *n*-type semiconductor are known as *donor impurities* because they donate or provide free electrons to the semiconductor crystal. In n-type, electrons are said to be the majority carriers whereas holes are the minority carriers.

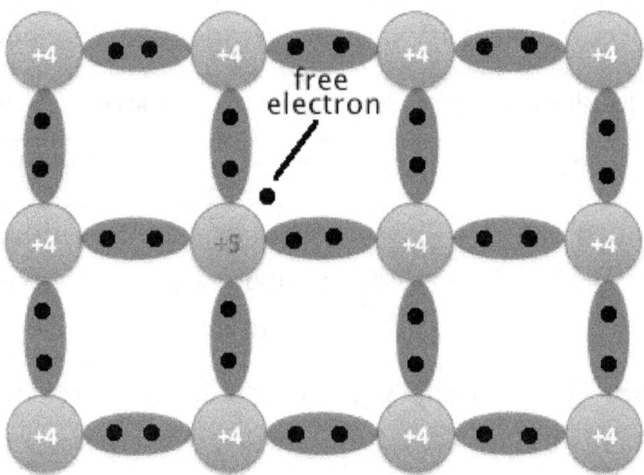

In the figure above Arsnic(+5) a penta valent impurity added to a tetra valent Silicon(+4). 4 electrons of Silicon combines with the 4 electrons of Arsnic and one free electron from of Arsnic leads to conduction

1.5 P-type Semiconductor

When a small amount of trivalent impurity is added to a pure semiconductor, it forms P-type Semiconductor.

The trivalent atom has three valence electrons and a pure semiconductor (tetravalent) atom have four valence electrons. The three valence electrons of the trivalent atom form covalent bonds with the neighboring tetravalent atoms. This leaves an empty space in the fourth covalent bond which is referred to as hole. When temperature is raised electron from another covalent bond jumps to fill this empty space. This leaves a hole behind. In this way conduction takes place.

Typical examples of trivalent impurities are *gallium, indium, boron etc*. Such impurities which produce *p*-type semiconductor are known as *acceptor impurities* because the holes created can accept the electrons. In P-type, electrons are said to be the minority carriers whereas holes are the majority carriers.

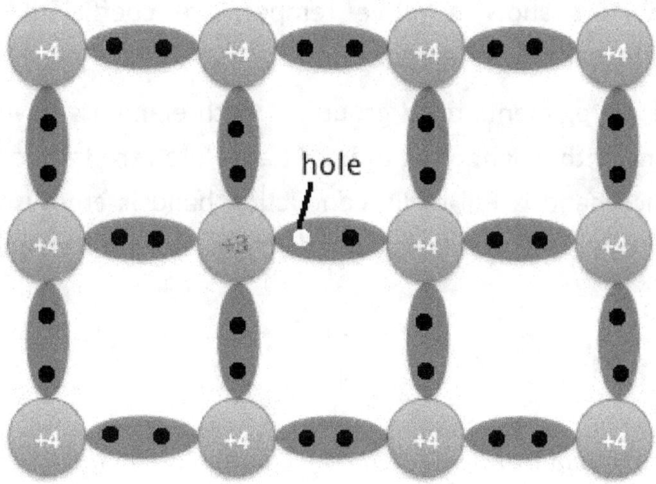

In the figure above Boron (+3) a tri valent impurity added to a tetra valent Silicon (+4). 3 electrons of Boron combine with the 3 electrons of Silicon and one gap hole is created which leads to conduction

1.6 Differences between N-Type and P-Type Extrinsic Semiconductors

The main differences between N-Type and P-Type extrinsic semiconductors are as follows

N-Type Extrinsic Semiconductors	P-Type Extrinsic Semiconductors
When a small amount of pentavalent impurity is added to a pure semiconductor, it forms N-type semiconductor	When a small amount of trivalent impurity is added to a pure semiconductor, it forms P-type Semiconductor
pentavalent impurities are *arsenic, antimony, Bismuth and Phosphorous etc*	trivalent impurities are *gallium, indium, boron etc*
The impurity atoms added, provide extra electrons in the structure and are called	The impurity atoms added, create vaccines (i.e. holes) in the structure and are called

donor atoms	acceptor atoms
Here electrons are majority carriers	Here holes are majority carriers
Here holes are minority carriers	Here electrons are minority carriers

1.7 Effect of Temperature on Semiconductors

At room temperature resistivity of semiconductor is in between insulators and conductors. Semiconductors show negative temperature coefficient of resistivity i.e. its resistance decreases with increase in temperature.

Both Si and Ge are elements of IV group i.e. both elements have 4 valence electrons. Both form covalent bond with neighboring atom. At absolute zero temperature both behave as insulator i.e. the valence band is full while conduction band is empty but as temperature is raised more and more covalent bonds break and electrons are set free and jump to conduction band.

Points to Remember

- ☞ *Semiconductors contain two types of mobile charge carriers, **Holes** and **Electrons**. The holes are positively charged while the electrons negatively charged.*
- ☞ *A semiconductor in an extremely pure form is known as an intrinsic semiconductor. Here flow of electron takes place by increasing the temperature*
- ☞ *A doped semiconductor or a semiconductor with suitable impurity atoms added to it is called extrinsic semiconductor. Extrinsic semiconductor are of two types : N-type and P-type.*
- ☞ *When a pure semiconductor of Ge or Si is doped with a controlled amount of pentavalent atoms, say arsenic or phosphorous or antimony or bismuth. We get N-type semiconductor or donor type semiconductor.*
- ☞ *It is called n-type semiconductor because the conduction of electricity in such semiconductor is due to motion of electrons i.e., negative charges, or n-type carriers. It is called donor type, because the doped impurity atom donates one free electron to semiconductor for conduction.*
- ☞ *In n-type semiconductor electrons are majority carriers and holes are minority carriers.*
- ☞ *When a pure semiconductor of Ge or Si is doped with a controlled amount of trivalent atoms, say indium or boron or aluminium, we get p-type semiconductor or acceptor type semiconductor.*

☞ *It is called p-type because the conduction of electricity in such semiconductors is due to motion of holes i.e., positive charges. It is called acceptor type semiconductor because the doped impurity atom creates a hole in semiconductor which accepts the electron, resulting conduction in p-type semiconductor.*

☞ *In p-type semiconductor, holes are majority carriers and electrons are minority carriers.*

1.8 PN Junction Diode

A diode is a simple electrical device that allows the flow of current in only one direction. It is derived from "di-ode " which means a device having two electrodes. The symbol of a p-n junction diode is shown below, the arrowhead points in the direction of conventional current flow.

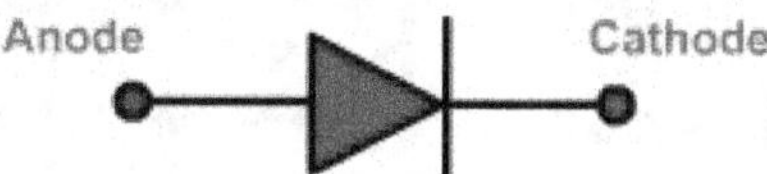

1.8.1 Formation of PN Junction Diode

The PN junction is a basic building block in any semiconductor device. It is formed by joining a P type and N type semiconductor together with a special fabrication technique such that a PN junction is formed. Hence it is a device with two elements, the P-type forms anode and the N-type forms the cathode. These terminals are brought out to make the external connections.

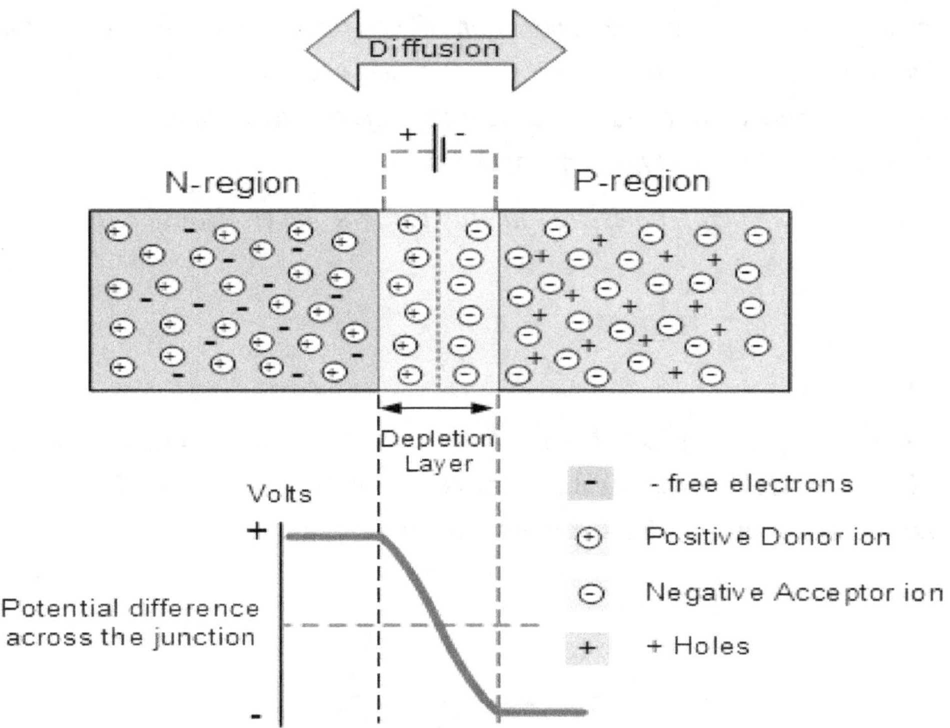

After joining P-type and N-type semiconductors, the N side will have large number of electrons and very few holes (due to thermal excitation) whereas the P side will have large number of holes and very few electrons. Due to this a process called diffusion takes place.

In this *diffusion process* free electrons from the N side will diffuse (spread) into the P side and combine with holes present there, leaving a positive immobile (not moveable) ion in the N side. Hence few atoms on the P side are converted into negative ions. Similarly few atoms on the n-side will get converted to positive ions. Due to this, large number of positive ions and negative ions will accumulate on the N-side and P-side respectively. This region so formed is called as *depletion region*.

Due to the presence of these positive and negative ions a static electric field called as *"barrier potential"* is created across the PN junction of the diode. It is called as "barrier potential" because it acts as a barrier and opposes the flow of positive and negative ions across the junction.

1.9 Diode Biasing

To make use of this PN junction diode we have to apply an external DC voltage to it. Applying an external DC voltage to the diode is called as biasing. There are two ways in which we can bias a PN junction diode.

> ➢ Forward bias

➢ Reverse bias

If the P-side (anode) is connected to the positive terminal of the supply and the N-side (cathode) to the negative terminal of the supply, the diode is said to be forward biased.

In the same way if the N-side is connected to the positive terminal of the supply and the P-side to the negative terminal of the supply, the diode is said to be reversed biased.

Most of the times a resistance have to be connected in series with it to limit the current flowing through the diode.

1.9.1 Forward Biased Condition

During forward biased, P-type (anode) is connected to the positive terminal of the supply and the N-type (cathode) to the negative terminal as shown in the below figure. The electrons from the N-type are repelled with the negative terminal of the supply and pushed towards the junction. Similarly holes from the P-type are repelled with the positive terminal of the supply and pushed towards the junction. Hence width of the depletion region starts reducing due to reduction in the barrier potential. This keeps happening and at a certain point the depletion region collapses and there is no opposition to the flow of current. Hence large number of electrons and holes will cross the junction and make the current to flow from anode to cathode.

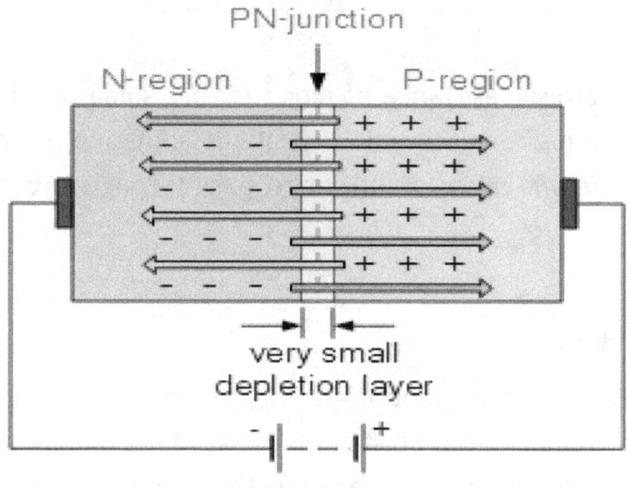

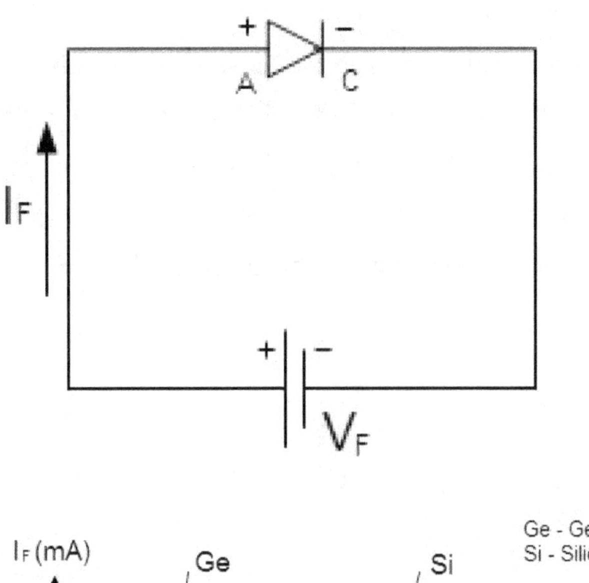

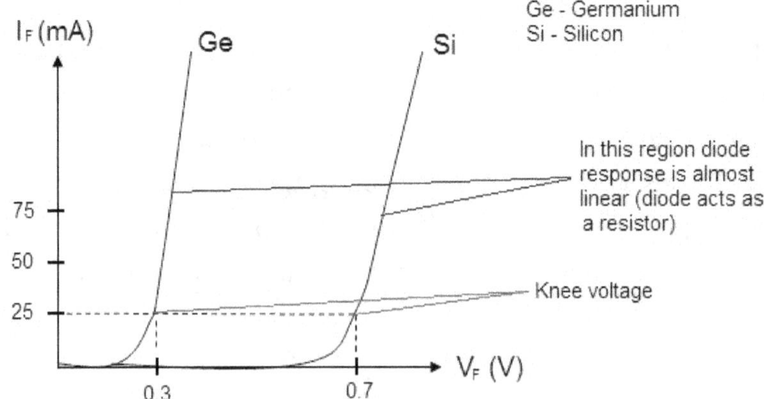

Forward biased electrical resistance of diode is very small and hence there is a small voltage drop across it. Its value for silicon diode is about 0.7 V and germanium is about 0.3V. Thus the PN junction diode will allow a current to pass through it only when it is forward biased.

1.9.2 Reverse Biased Condition

During reverse biased, P-type (anode) is connected to the negetive terminal of the supply and the N-type (cathode) to the positive terminal of the supply as shown in the below figure. The electrons from the N-type are attracted with the positive terminal of the supply and pushed away from the junction. Similarly holes from the P-type are attracted with the negative terminal of the supply and pushed away from the junction. Hence width of the depletion region starts increasing. This keeps happening providing high resistance and opposes the flow of current. Hence electrons and holes will not cross the junction.

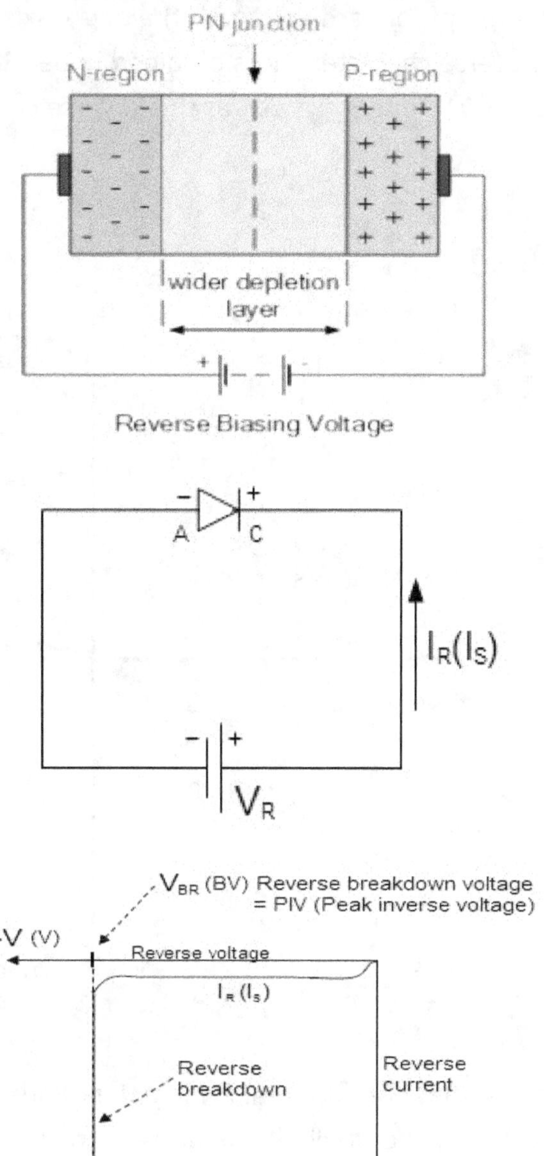

Hence, ideally the reverse biased resistance of the diode is infinite and no current flows from the diode when it is reversed biased. Due to large reverse biased voltage, suddenly large current will flow through the reverse biased voltage. Due to this large power gets dissipated in the diode which may damage it permanently.

1.9.3 V-I Characteristics of Diode

The V-I characteristic of a diode is the forward and reverse characteristics of a PN junction diode as shown in the below figure. Forward characteristic is obtained under forward bias condition and is the graph of forward voltage (Vf) along x-axis versus the forward current (If) along y-axis. Similarly Reverse characteristic is obtained under Reverse bias condition and is the graph of Reverse voltage (Vr) along x-axis versus the Reverse current (Ir) along y-axis.

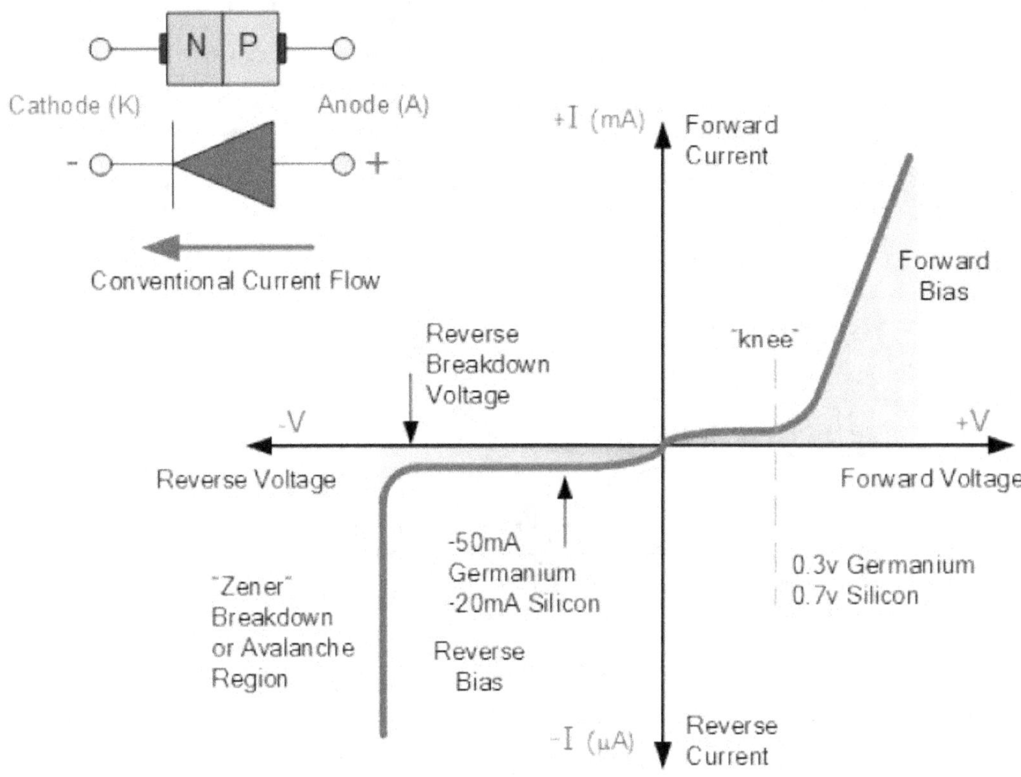

Under forward biased condition of a real PN junction diode, current flows from P to N-type in forward direction. When the applied voltage is more than the barrier potential, the resistance is small (ideally 0) and the current increases rapidly. This point is called the *Knee-point* or *turn-on voltage* or *threshold voltage*. This voltage is about 0.3 volts for Ge diodes and 0.7 volts for Si diodes.

Under reverse biased condition, increasing the potential barrier due to which no current should flow ideally. But in practice, the minority carriers can travel down the potential barrier to give very small current. This is called as the *reverse saturation current*. This current is about 50µA for Ge diodes and 20µA for Si diodes.

However, if the reverse bias is made too high, the current through the PN junction increases abruptly. The voltage at which this phenomenon occurs is known as the *breakdown or reverse breakdown voltage*.

1.9.4 PN Junction Diode Equation

The p-n junction diode current equation can be represented by Shockley's equation as given below

$$I_D = I_S(e^{V_D/nV_T} - 1)$$

Here, I_D = Diode current

I_s = reverse saturation current

V_D = Voltage drop across diode

n = emission co-efficient, which is a number between 1 and 2, which typically increases as the current increases.

$$V_T = kT/q,$$

where k is Boltzmann's constant,

q is the charge on an electron and

T is the temperature in Kelvin.

1.9.5 Effect of Temperature on Diode Current

Temperature can have considerable effect on the characteristics of diode. In the diode current

$$I_D = I_S(e^{V_D/nV_T} - 1)$$

Consider the term V_T given in above equation. This term is called thermal voltage and is dependent on temperature by the relation $V_T = kT/q$. This term indirectly suggests the dependence of diode characteristics on temperature.

Effect of temperature on forward characteristics

The characteristics curve of a Si diode shifts to the left at the rate of -2.5 mV per degree centigrade change in temperature in forward bias region.

For example if the temperature increases from room temperature (25° C) to 80° C, the voltage drop across the diode will be (80-25) x 2.5 mV = 137.5 mV.

Effect of temperature on reverse characteristics

In the reverse bias region, the reverse saturation current of Si and Ge diodes doubles for every 10° C rise in temperature.

Let us take an example to understand how much the reverse saturation current changes with temperature. Consider an increase of temperature from 25 °C to 85 °C, where the reverse saturation current at 25 °C is 100 nA. The temperature increases by 60 °C (25 °C to 85 °C), which is 6 x 10. Hence the reverse saturation current would increase by a factor of $2^6 = 64$. Hence the reverse saturation current at 85 °C will be 100 nA x 64 = 6400 nA.

A graph showing the variation of reverse saturation current with temperature is shown below. The difference between the curve is exaggerated for illustration purpose.

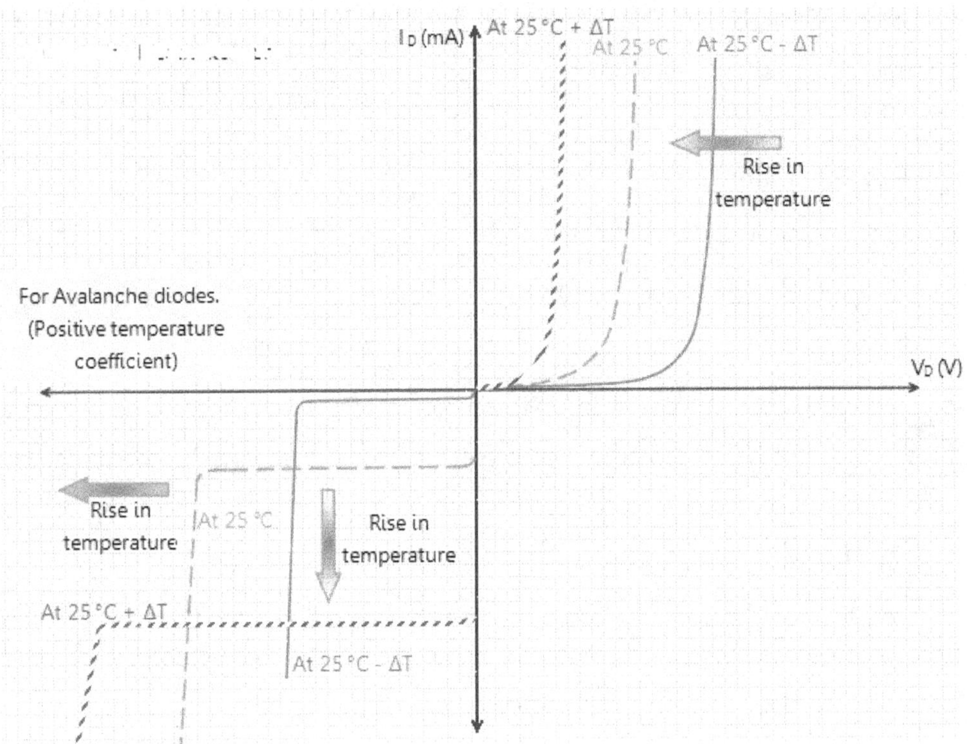

From the above graph it is clear that the reverse saturation current increases with increase in temperature. The graph also shows how the reverse breakdown voltage changes with temperature. It is indicated in the above graph that the reverse breakdown voltage increases with an increase in temperature.

1.10 Ratings/Specifications of a Diode

The main basic ratings of the diode are as follows

- ☞ Knee voltage or Cut-in Voltage.
- ☞ Breakdown voltage
- ☞ Peak-inverse voltage (PIV)
- ☞ Maximum Forward current

☞ Maximum Power rating

Knee voltage or Cut-in Voltage: It is the forward voltage at which the diode starts conducting.

Breakdown voltage: It is the reverse voltage at which the diode (PN junction) breaks down with sudden rise in reverse current.

Peak-inverse voltage (PIV): It is the maximum reverse voltage that can be applied to a PN junction without causing damage to the junction.

If the reverse voltage across the junction exceeds its peak-inverse voltage, then the junction gets destroyed because of excessive heat.

Maximum Forward current: It is the maximum instantaneous forward current that a PN junction can conduct without damaging the junction. If the forward current is more than the specified rating then the junction gets destroyed due to overheating.

Maximum Power rating: It is the maximum power that can be dissipated at the junction without damaging it. The power dissipated across the junction is equal to the product of junction current and the voltage across the junction.

1.11 Ideal and Real view of a Diode

We can approximate the characteristic of diode by replacing the diode in the circuit with its equivalent circuit. An equivalent circuit is nothing but a combination of elements that best represents the actual terminal characteristics of the device. In simple language, it simply means the diode in the circuit can be replaced by other elements without severely affecting the behavior of circuit.

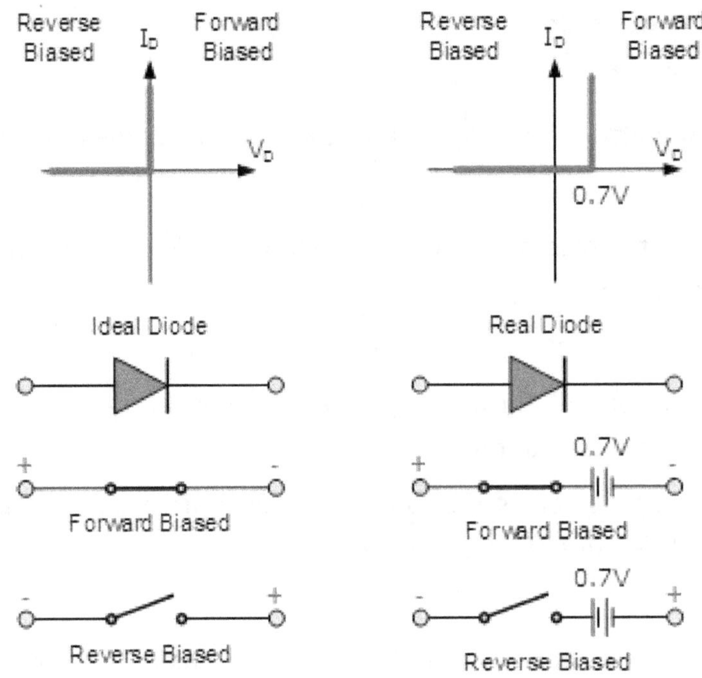

1.12 Applications of PN Junction Diode

PN Junction diode can be found in several applications. Some of these are:

- ☞ Can be used as rectifier in DC Power Supplies
- ☞ In Demodulation or Detector Circuits
- ☞ In clamping networks used as DC Restorers
- ☞ In clipping circuits used for waveform generation.
- ☞ As switches in digital logic circuits.

1.12.1 Diode as a Switch

The simplest application of a diode is the switch shown in the below figure

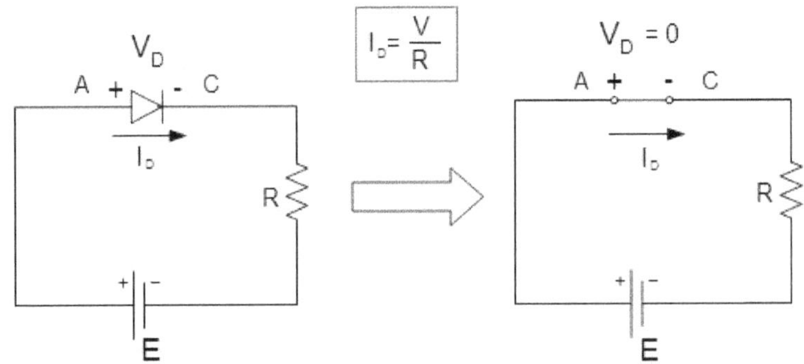

Forward Biased diode looks like a "short circuit" or closed switch. When the input to this circuit is at potential shown in the above figure, the diode conducts and acts as a straight piece of wire because of its very low forward resistance. In effect, it forms a path as closed switch to reach the load resistor. Therefore, the diode, acts as a closed switch when its anode is positive with respect to its cathode.

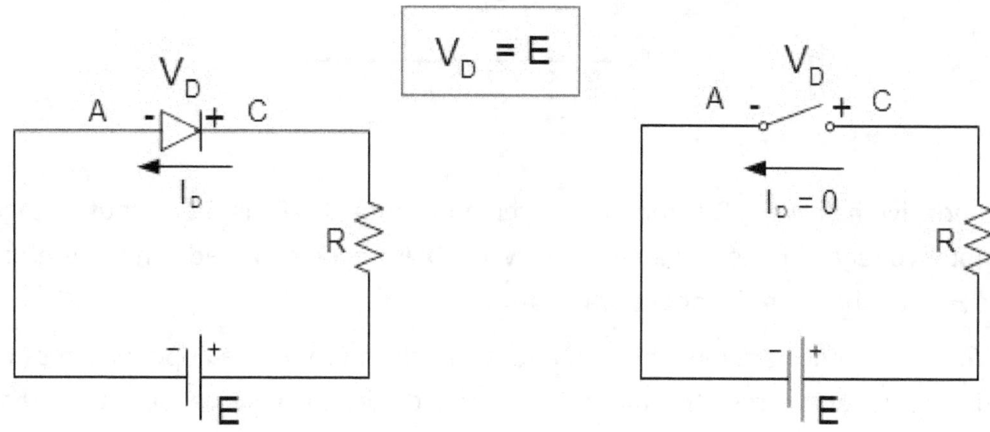

Reverse biased diode looks like an "open circuit" or open switch. When the input to this circuit is at potential shown in the above figure, the diode does not conducts and acts as a broken piece of wire because of its very high reverse resistance. In effect, it does not forms a path as by open switch to reach the load resistor. Therefore, the diode, acts as a open switch when its anode is negative with respect to its cathode.

1.12.2 Diode as Half Wave Rectifier:

Rectification is the conversion of alternating current (AC) to direct current (DC). This involves a device that only allows one-way flow of electrons. The simplest kind of rectifier circuit is the *half-wave* rectifier. It only allows one half of an AC waveform to pass through to the load.

The single – phase half wave rectifier is shown in the below figure. It consists of a step down transformer, diode and a load resistor. The diode will be ON for half cycle and OFF for another half cycle.

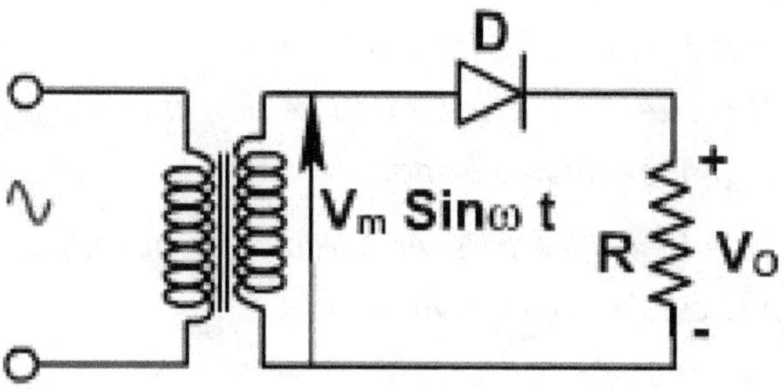

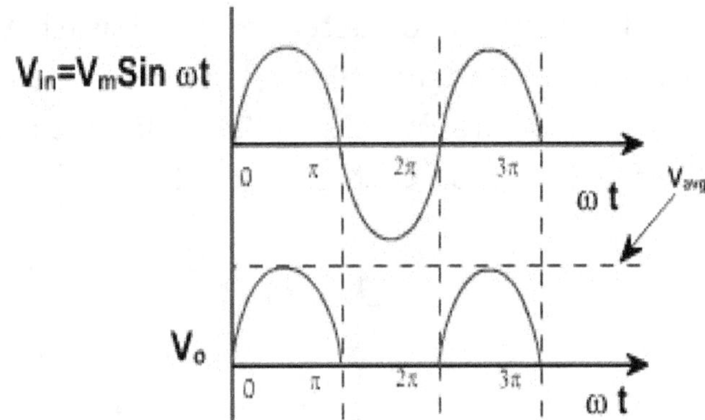

In positive half cycle, D is forward biased and conducts. Thus the output voltage is same as the input voltage. In the negative half cycle, D is reverse biased, and therefore output voltage is zero as shown in the above waveform.

When the diode is reverse biased, entire transformer voltage appears across the diode. The maximum voltage across the diode is V_m. The diode must be capable to withstand this voltage.

Points to remember

☞ *When a p-type crystal is brought into close contact with n-type crystal, the resulting arrangement is called p - n junction or junction diode.*

☞ *Depletion region is a layer created around the junction which is devoid of free charge carriers and has immobile ions.*

☞ *When positive terminal of external battery is connected to p-side and negative to n-side of p-n junction, the p-n junction is said to be forward biased.*

☞ *In forward biasing, the conduction across p-n junction takes place due to migration of majority carriers (i.e. electrons from n-side to p-side and holes from p-sides to n-side). The size of the depletion region decreases. The resistance of p-n junction becomes low.*

☞ *A p-n junction is said to be reverse biased if the positive terminal of the external battery is connected to n-side and the negative terminal to p-side of p-n junction.*

☞ *In reverse biasing, the conduction across the p-n junction does not takes place due to majority carriers but takes place due to minority carriers if the voltage of external battery is large. The size of the depletion region increase. The resistance of the p-n junction becomes high in reverse biasing.*

☞ *Forward Biased diode looks like a "short circuit" or closed switch. Reverse biased diode looks like an "open circuit" or open switch.*

☞ *Rectification is the conversion of alternating current (AC) to pulsating direct current (DC). This involves a device that only allows one-way flow of electrons. The simplest kind of rectifier circuit is the half-wave rectifier. It only allows one half of an AC waveform to pass through to the load.*

1.13 Zener diode

Zener diodes are a special kind of diode where it is possible to build a special type that can handle breakdown without failing completely. Its symbol looks like as shown in the below figure

When forward-biased, zener diodes behave much the same as standard rectifying diodes: they have a forward voltage drop which follows the "diode equation" and is about 0.7 volts.

In reverse-bias mode, they do not conduct until the applied voltage reaches or exceeds the so-called *zener voltage*, at which point the diode is able to conduct substantial current, and in doing so will try to limit the voltage dropped across it to that zener voltage point. So long as the power dissipated by this reverse current does not exceed the diode's thermal limits, the diode will not be harmed.

Zener diodes are manufactured with zener voltages ranging anywhere from a few volts to hundreds of volts. This zener voltage changes slightly with temperature

The point at which the zener voltage triggers the current to flow through the diode can be very accurately controlled in the doping stage of the diodes semiconductor construction giving the diode a specific *zener breakdown voltage*, (V_z) for example, 4.3V or 7.5V. This zener breakdown voltage on the V-I curve is almost a vertical straight line.

1.13.1 V-I Characteristics of Zener Diode

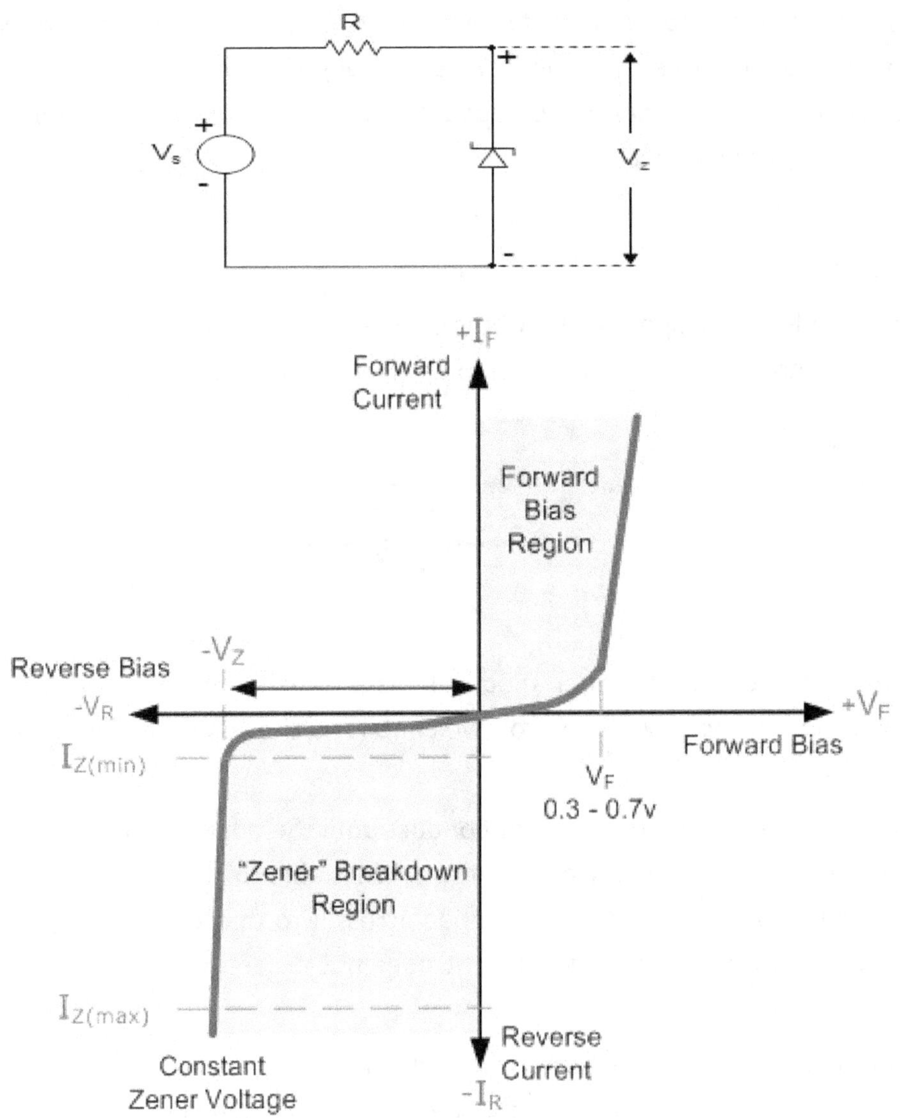

The Zener Diode is used in its "reverse bias" or reverse breakdown mode, i.e. the diodes anode connects to the negative terminal of the supply and cathode connects to positive terminal of the supply. From the V-I characteristics curve above, we can see that the zener diode has a region in its reverse bias characteristics of almost a constant negative voltage regardless of the value of the current flowing through the diode and remains nearly constant even with large changes in current as long as the zener diodes current remains between the breakdown current $I_{Z(min)}$ and the maximum current rating $I_{Z(max)}$. The reverse breakdown voltage of the Zener diode is set by carefully controlling the doping level during the manufacturing process. Zener diodes are very heavily doped to reduce the breakdown voltage, causing very narrow depletion layer.

Zener Diode has two types of reverse breakdown. They are:

☞ Avalanche breakdown

☞ Zener breakdown

Zener diodes with breakdown voltages of less than approximately 5V operate predominantly in Zener breakdown. Those diodes with the breakdown voltage greater than 5V operate predominantly in avalanche breakdown. Both types are called Zener diodes and are commercially available with breakdown voltages from 1.8V all the way to 200V.

1.13.2 Avalanche breakdown

We know that when the diode is reverse biased a small reverse saturation current flows across the junction because of the minority carriers in the depletion region.

The velocity of the minority charge carriers is directly proportional to the applied voltage. Hence when the reverse bias voltage is increased, the velocity of minority charge carriers will also increase and consequently their energy content will also increase.

When these high energy charge carriers strikes the atom within the depletion region they cause other charge carriers to break away from their atoms and join the flow of current across the junction. The additional charge carriers generated in this way strikes other atoms and generate new carriers by making them to break away from their atoms.

This cumulative process is referred to as avalanche multiplication which results in the flow of large reverse current and this breakdown of the diode is called avalanche breakdown.

1.13.3 Zener breakdown

We have electric field strength = Reverse voltage/ Depletion region

From the above relation we see that the reverse voltage is directly proportional to the electric field hence, a small increase in reverse voltage produces a very high intensity electric field within a narrow Depletion region.

Therefore in Zener breakdown when the reverse voltage of a diode is increased, the electrostatic attraction between the negative electrons and a large positive voltage is so great that it pulls electrons out of their covalent bonds and away from their parent atoms. ie Electrons are transferred from the valence to the conduction band. In this situation the current can still be limited by the limited number of free electrons produced by the applied voltage so it is possible to cause Zener breakdown without damaging the semiconductor.

1.14 Applications of Zener diode

Zener diodes can be found in several applications. Some of these are:

☞ Voltage stabilizers or regulators (in shunt mode)

☞ Surge suppressors for device protection

☞ Peak clippers

☞ Switching operations

☞ Reference elements and in meter protection applications

The constant reverse voltage of a Zener diode renders it a very useful component in regulating the output voltage against variations in the load resistance or variations in the input voltage from an unregulated power supply. The current through the Zener diode will change in order to keep the voltage within the threshold limits of Zener action and the maximum power that it can dissipate.

1.14.1 Zener Diode as a Voltage Regulator

Zener Diodes can be used to produce a stabilized voltage output with low ripple under varying load current conditions as shown in the below figure

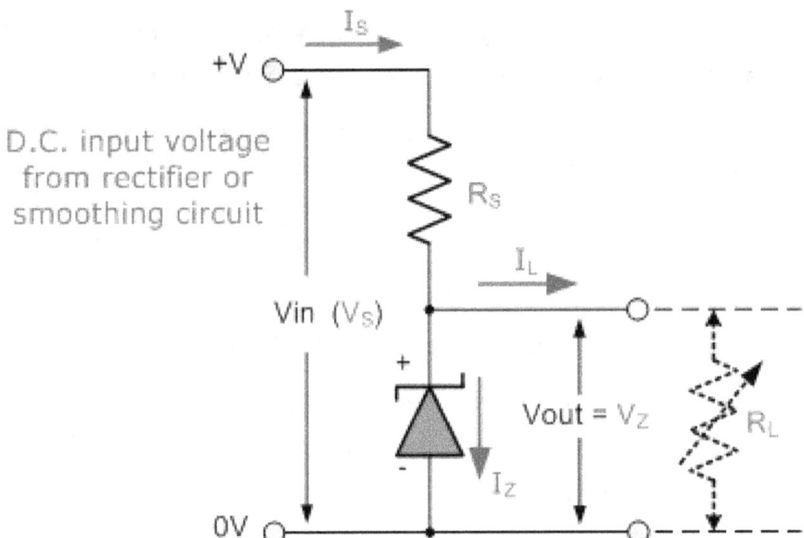

The resistor, R_S is connected in series with the zener diode to limit the current flow through the diode with the voltage source, V_S being connected across the combination. The stabilised output voltage V_{out} is taken across the zener diode. The zener diode is connected with its cathode terminal connected to the positive rail of the DC supply so it is reverse biased and will be operating in its breakdown condition.

With no load connected to the circuit, the load current will be zero, ($I_L = 0$), and all the circuit current passes through the zener diode which in turn dissipates its maximum power.

With load connected in parallel with the zener diode, the voltage across R_L is always the same as the zener voltage, ($V_R = V_Z$). There is a minimum zener current for which the stabilization of the voltage is effective and the zener current must stay above this value operating under load within its breakdown region at all times. The upper limit of current is of course dependent upon the power rating of the device. The supply voltage V_S must be greater than V_Z.

Hence in short, a zener diode is always operated in its reverse biased condition. A voltage regulator circuit can be designed using a zener diode to maintain a constant DC output voltage across the load in spite of variations in the input voltage or changes in the load current. The zener voltage regulator consists of a current limiting resistor R_S connected in series with the input voltage V_S with the zener diode connected in parallel with the load R_L in this reverse biased condition. The stabilized output voltage is always selected to be the same as the breakdown voltage V_Z of the diode.

Points to remember

☞ *Zener diodes behave much the same as standard rectifying diodes during forward biased. In reverse-bias mode, they do not conduct until the applied voltage reaches or exceeds the so-called zener voltage*

☞ *Zener diodes with breakdown voltages of less than approximately 5V operate predominantly in Zener breakdown. Those diodes with the breakdown voltage greater than 5V operate predominantly in avalanche breakdown*

☞ *Zener Diodes can be used to produce a stabilized voltage output with low ripple under varying load current conditions*

Review Questions

1) Explain the Atomic Structure
2) State and explain the Neil Bohr's Atomic Theory
3) Explain the energy band diagram
4) Define the following
   a) Conduction band
   b) Valence band
   c) Forbidden band
5) Explain conductors, insulators and semiconductors with energy level diagram
6) Mention the properties of semiconductors
7) Mention the differences between conductors, insulators and semiconductors
8) Give the classification of semiconductors

9) Explain intrinsic and extrinsic semiconductors with examples

10) Mention the differences between Intrinsic and Extrinsic Semiconductors

11) Explain the structure of N-type semiconductor

12) Explain the structure of P-type semiconductor

13) Mention the differences between N-Type and P-Type Extrinsic Semiconductors

14) Define the following

    a) Doping

    b) Dopant

    c) PN Junction Diode

    d) Diode Biasing

    e) Zener Diode

15) Discriminate between

    a) Pentavalent and Trivalent dopants

    b) Majority and Minority charge carriers

    c) Donor and acceptor

16) Explain the effect of temperature on Semiconductors

17) Describe the formation of PN junction, depletion region and potential barrier

18) Describe forward and reverse biasing of a PN junction diode

19) Demonstrate the V-I characteristics of PN junction diode

    Or Demonstrate the Forward and Reverse characteristics of PN junction diode

20) Write the PN Junction Diode Equation

21) Discuss the effect of temperature on barrier voltage in PN junction diode

22) List and define the specifications of a Diode

23) Analyze the Ideal and Real view of a Diode

24) Mention the applications of PN Junction Diode

25) Illustrate a PN junction diode as a switch

26) Illustrate a PN junction diode as a half wave rectifier

27) Describe the working of zener diode in forward and reverse bias condition

28) Define Avalanche breakdown and Zener breakdown. Give the differences between them

29) Demonstrate the V-I characteristics of zener diode

30) Mention the applications of Zener diode

31) Illustrate a zener diode as a voltage regulator

www.ingramcontent.com/pod-product-compliance
Lightning Source LLC
Chambersburg PA
CBHW081408130726
47998CB00011B/3120